SOCK MONKEYS
SOCK MONKEYS
SOCK MONKEYS
ACTIVITY BOOK

by

Dee Lindner

A 'Brainy' Socktastic Keepsake

9 8 7 6 5 4 3 2 1

ISBN 978-1-986637-37-4

COPYRIGHT 2018 © DEE LINDNER

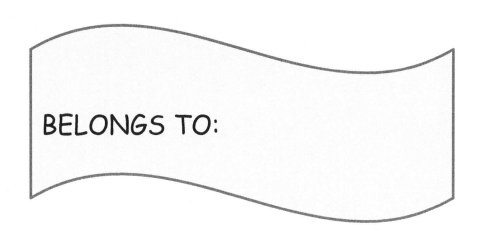

BELONGS TO:

 To Gary

My Big Brain

Visit WWW.SOCKMONKEYLADY.COM

For *Sockdillyumptuous* Monkey Muse
& Whimsical Gifts

FOREWORD

Dear Reader,

When Dee Lindner, the Sock Monkey Lady®, asked if I would endorse her book, I envisioned sock monkeys jumping from its pages in playful parody of life. How could I resist the opportunity to promote the art of play in an entertaining, educational activity book? You see, the Sock Monkey Lady thinks of me as the "King of Play," and truth be told, she knows that I truly am a big kid at heart who promotes free play in any learning form.

```
SOCK MONKEYS
SOCK MONKEYS
SOCK MONKEYS
ACTIVITY BOOK
```

As a businessman and philanthropist, I have dedicated years of my life in fostering safe environments where children can be creative in play, and escape the rigors of everyday strife. To this end, or should I say beginning, I founded Kids Around the World and have built playgrounds in communities where kids can exercise their imaginations and experience the simple, good things in life while developing physical and social skills.

Similarly, the Sock Monkey Lady has dedicated her life's work to the art of make-believe by promoting the Red-heel Sock Monkey Tradition—a tradition teeming with sentimental stories of children and adults who have found sock monkeys to be a creative, nurturing outlet of intrinsic value.

Is it any wonder that playscapes contain monkey bars? Sock monkeys and playgrounds are synonymous with the word 'fun'. They both represent make-believe at its best. For whom can resist playgrounds and best pals that induce adventure and laughter? They are citadels that silently nurture and shape young minds that will one day be integral to the machinations of our world as artisans, journeymen, businessmen, parents, world leaders, etc.

But what really tickles my socks off is that the origin of red-heel sock monkeys started right here in my own hometown, Rockford, Illinois— Home of the Sock Monkey. So it is with enthusiasm, that I invite young and old alike, to sharpen their pencils and their wits and let the fun begin by solving a variety of creative activities in Dee's latest book, a page-turner where sock monkeys reign in the playground of life!

Dennis Johnson
Founder, Chairman of Kids Around the World
Rockford University, Trustee
Board Member of David C. Cook
President of Bibles for Kids
President of Stockholm Inn

INTRODUCTION

Inside you will discover one of the coolest activity books—great for honing motor skills (coloring and drawing) to critical thinking and more! Stuffed with *sock foolery* of varying skill levels, sock monkeys take center stage in activities that will razzle dazzle young and old alike.

Perfect for travel, home, or school, this book is chockfull of hours of fun where one can unravel while learning about the iconic Red-heel Sock Monkey Tradition born in the USA.

The foreword by Dennis Johnson, from Rockford, Illinois—where the original red-heel socks were manufactured—is heartwarming. As Founder/Chairman of Kids Around the World, his love for playscapes and sock monkeys come together amidst pages where both fun and learning abound!

> SOCK MONKEYS
> SOCK MONKEYS
> SOCK MONKEYS
> **ACTIVITY BOOK**
>
> SHENANIGANS INCLUDE
>
> | | |
> |---|---|
> | •What's missing | •Mazes |
> | •Fill in the blank | •Word search |
> | •Color | •Dot-to-dot |
> | •Sketch | •Pages to color |
> | •Decode | •Unscramble |
> | •Multiple choice | •Fun facts |
> | •Jokes | •Match |

Whether you are a big or little brain, relax, get ready to monkey around, and join in the magic of sock monkey fun and play! Not sure of your brainpower? Answers can be found in the back of the book.

Dee Lindner
Sock Monkey Lady®

THE MAGIC OF
SOCK MONKEYS,
FUN & PLAY

1. Rockford,
   Illinois, USA
   is 'Home of the
   Sock Monkey'.

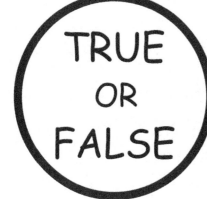

TRUE
OR
FALSE

2. The name of the first
   knitting company that
   manufactured the original
   red-heel socks was Nelson
   Knitting Company (NKC).

SOCK MONKEY PARTS

Match each area of this pair of red-heel socks to its monkey part.
Write the number of your answer on the corresponding line provided.

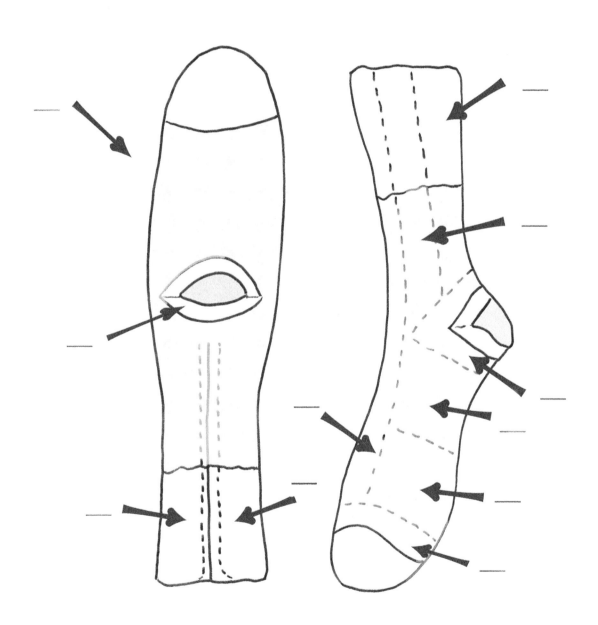

1. Main body
2. Leg A
3. Leg B
4. Bum
5. Arm A
6. Arm B
7. Tail
8. Ear A
9. Ear B
10. Mouth piece
11. Hat

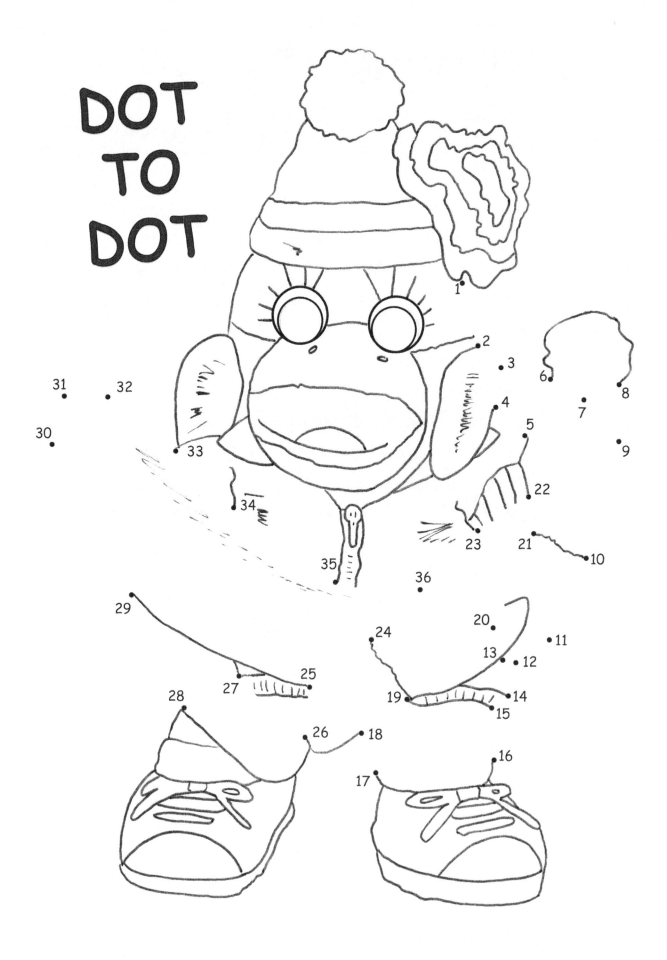

DOT
TO
DOT

COLOR
BY
NUMBER

1 - Yellow
2 - Red
3 - Cream
4 - Brown
5 - Light blue
6 - Purple
7 - Dark blue
8 - Black
9 - Green

SOCK MONKEY & PLAYGROUND ORIGINS

1. WHO WAS ONE OF THE KEY PLAYERS IN THE INVENTION OF THE FIRST PRACTICAL AUTOMATED HOSIERY KNITTING MACHINE BEHIND OUR FAMED RED-HEEL SOCKS?

   A. NELSON MONK   B. JOHN NELSON   C. NELLIE'S SEWING BEE

THE FOUNDATION FOR PLAYGROUNDS BEGAN AS SAND GARDENS (SAND LOTS). SAND GARDENS ARE SAID TO HAVE BEEN INTRODUCED IN GERMANY IN 1850 FOR CHILDREN'S PLAY. BY 1899 THERE WERE 21 SAND GARDENS IN THE UNITED STATES.

2. WHEN DID THE ORIGINAL RED-HEEL SOCKS FIRST BECOME AVAILABLE?

   A. LAST VALENTINE'S DAY   B. BEFORE TEDDY BEARS   C. 1932

THE 'PLAYGROUND ASSOCIATION OF AMERICA' WAS FOUNDED IN 1906 — ITS SUBJECT RECREATION. THE INSTITUTE IS NOW KNOWN AS THE 'NATIONAL RECREATION AND PARK ASSOCIATION'.

3. WHAT WERE THE FIRST THREE COLORS OF THE ORIGINAL RED-HEEL SOCK?

    A. BRIGHT BLUE, CANARY YELLOW, AND WHITE
    B. BROWN HEATHER, CREAM, AND RED
    C. PURPLE DURPLE, BANANA YELLOW, AND RED

4. WHO MADE AMERICA'S FIRST RED-HEEL SOCK MONKEY?

    A. GRANDPA   B. SUZIE HOME-MAKER   C. UNKNOWN

WE DO NOT KNOW THE DATE OF WHEN THE FIRST RED-HEEL SOCK MONKEY WAS CREATED—BUT IT COULD HAVE BEEN AS EARLY AS 1932 WHEN THE RED-HEEL SOCKS BECAME AVAILABLE.

THE PATENT FOR THE SOCK MONKEY DOLL WAS OBTAINED BY KNC IN 1955.

5. FROM WHAT SOCK SIZES ARE MOST RED-HEEL SOCK MONKEYS TYPICALLY SEWN:

    A. SMALL
    B. MEDIUM
    C. LARGE
    D. EX-LARGE

COLOR THESE 'PLAY' PALS USING NKC'S INITIAL RED-HEEL SOCK COLORS!

6. WHAT MINIMAL NUMBER OF SOCKS IS REQUIRED TO CREATE A STANDARD-SIZED RED-HEEL SOCK MONKEY?

    A. SIX   B. TWO   C. FOUR

THE SOCK MONKEY LADY® CREATED THE *SOCKNORMOUS* 7'2" SOCK MONKEY NAMED 'NELSON' THAT RESIDES AT THE MIDWAY VILLAGE MUSEUM IN ROCKFORD, IL. NELSON IS MADE FROM 42 RED-HEEL SOCKS.

7. HOW LONG DOES IT TYPICALLY TAKE TO HAND-SEW A SOCK MONKEY WITH THE AID OF A SEWING MACHINE AND BASIC SEWING SKILLS?

    A. ONE-TWO WEEKS   B. ONE DAY   C. TWO-THREE HOURS

THE SOCK MONKEY LADY® CREATED 'NELSON' IN 44 HOURS

8. WHAT STYLE OF EYES ARE RECOMMENDED FOR SAFETY ON SOCK MONKEYS CREATED FOR SMALL CHILDREN?

    A. BUTTONS   B. FELT   C. JIGGLE   D. EMBROIDERED

9. WHAT WORD WOULD FIT A 'GROUP' OF SOCK MONKEYS BEST:

    A. HERD   B. BARREL   C. PECK

10. WHAT IS THE APPROXIMATE LENGTH OF A STANDARD-SIZED SOCK MONKEY FROM TOP OF HEAD TO BOTTOM OF FOOT?

    A. 28-36 INCHES   B. 18-24 INCHES   C. 10-12 INCHES

PLAYSCAPES ARE EVER CHANGING AND CAN BE FOUND WORLDWIDE. WHAT IS SAID TO BE THE TALLEST AND LONGEST TUNNEL SLIDE IS APPROXIMATELY 580 FEET LONG AND OPENED IN 2016 AT QUEEN ELIZABETH OLYMPIC PARK IN LONDON, ENGLAND.

11. WHAT AGE GROUP LOVES SOCK MONKEYS?

    A. ADULTS B. BOYS   C. GIRLS   D. BABIES   E. ALL THE ABOVE

12. WHY ARE SOCK MONKEYS SO POPULAR?

    A. FUN COLLECTIBLES   B. POWER TO NURTURE C. FUN PLAYMATES
    D. SUPPLEMENT INCOME   E. WIDELY AFFORDABLE   F. ALL THE ABOVE

13. WHAT IS A COMMON NAME FOR A SOCK MONKEY?

    A.   BOZO   B. ELMO   C. SOCKEY

14. WHAT EQUIPMENT WOULD 'SOCKEY' LIKE BEST AT PLAYGROUNDS?

    A. SLIDES   B. TILT-A-WHIRLS   C. MONKEY BARS

"It is a happy talent to know how to play."

- Ralph Waldo Emerson

RIDDLE FUN!

1. What type of key won't open a door?

2. Who should a monkey see when it loses its tail?

3. What does a monkey wear when it is cooking?

the
MONKEY BUZZ

```
C U B S O C K M O N K E Y S P N F I T T L A M N
F P I W E L B A G G U H O I R A L P H O A C Y E
S P G D U L R H I Y E D M A Z S O I R B Y O T S
N I G E T V O W L L A S Y B G T X K E S E D A O
G F R O C K F O R D I L L I N O I S A O J N E C
A O I F O S M I O D C A S O W T M E D K A S I K
S N N I S E I D D U B N D S G S O L Y C O T O P
N E S C S H E D A C L K N Q R F N A I Z P U R E
A S N O T T U B M O A Y E L U R E R Q O S F I N
G T U N I Q U E P S S L I N E H E I M L O F E D
I I N I R D E L R M A I R I V M S P F O S E N O
N T E C H E B N O T A M F T A Z O S U N E D P U
A C I D E F D O X O E B T E S M S A C E L W C S
N H F O I L L H B I L S S E S E J B E L B A S T
E A O L H R Z L E P I N E C L D D E K A I M E T
H T R S I H U G P E S S B I C R O E P N T A L E
S A H E O I Q L O E L I M S O C E L S M C H B S
O T H L G M A O E I T S T O A I F V L O E C A O
C I E S A Y I R A N Y I O K Q N S A E S L H E K
P M I S M P O T P N A K R C R E A N O R L I V N
L E S A W I G O N L S H T O K J U N T F O S O I
I X T T A N T U R C U O G O V S S O A M C F L W
C E Z P O L S E D A M D N A H A Q I K B T H E C
S T Y L B O R N I N T H E U S A F P E V O T A H
L S O I T H R E N D U N I S P E A E G Z H G P O
T C Y N A P M O C G N I T T I N K N O S L E N E
H R N S O C P S O C H K P A R L I T W Z M A L W
```

SOCK MONKEYS	BUDDIES	POMPOMS
BORN IN THE USA	FAVORITE	ICONIC
HAND MADE	PLAYMATES	DOLLS
ONE STITCH AT A TIME	LOVEABLE	GO BANANAS
NELSON KNITTING COMPANY	BEST FRIENDS	HEIRLOOMS
ROCKFORD ILLINOIS	FUN	AMERICANA
THREADY	SHENANIGANS	FOREVER
RED HEEL SOCKS	HUGGABLE	
SOFT	CUDDLY	
BIG GRINS	HOT COLLECTIBLES	
SUNNY SMILES	STUFFED	
LANKY LIMBS	TOY	
LONG TAILS	BUTTONS	
UNIQUE	YARN	
SOCKPENDOUS	TASSLES	

FIND EIGHT FUN THINGS TO DO AT A PLAYGROUND

WORD SEARCH

M	O	C	R	A	W	L	J
A	P	L	I	T	S	D	U
S	L	I	D	E	P	A	M
W	E	M	Y	G	I	S	P
I	F	B	O	U	N	C	E
N	E	L	R	I	G	J	S
G	H	A	N	G	E	T	N

Swing   Hang
Slide   Crawl
Spin   Jump
Climb   Bounce

RAISE THE MONKEY BAR!

Learn fun words
to use from the
Sock Monkey Lady's
sockopedia!

KEY:

A B C D E F G H I J K L M N O P Q R S T U V W X Y Z

1 2 3 4 5 6 7 8 9 10 11 12 13 14 15 16 17 18 19 20 21 22 23 24 25 26

19, 15, 3, 11, 16, 5, 14, 4, 15, 21, 19

19, 15, 3, 11, 20, 1, 19, 20, 9, 3

19, 15, 3, 11, 19, 9, 12, 12, 25, 21, 13, 16, 20, 21,15, 21,19

19, 15, 3, 11, 9, 20, 9, 26, 5

19, 15, 3, 11, 21, 12, 5, 14, 20

19, 15, 3, 11, 19, 1, 20, 9, 15, 14, 1, 12

Make up a word of your own!

PLAYSCAPES OFTEN INCLUDE GREENSPACES FOR ADDED FUN!

Rearrange the scrambled letters to reveal the hidden words!

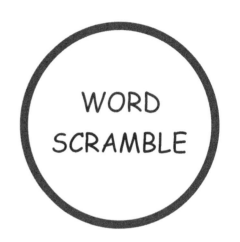

WORD SCRAMBLE

_____	LALABESB
_____	GTA
_____	SKARCCSAE (2 WORDS)
_____	CCESOR
_____	UHCTOOLTBLFAO (TWO WORDS)
_____	ATNMIBDNO
_____	YLVELBLLOA
_____	FFNANBDILMSBUL (TWO WORDS)
_____	HSRCWATLEE
_____	NEDHEIESKDA (THREE WORDS)

FIND THE
DIFFERENCES

These two pictures look
exactly alike, but look again.
Can you find nine places where
they are different?

MONKEY SHINES!

WHAT DO SOCK MONKEYS & PLAYGROUNDS HAVE IN COMMON?

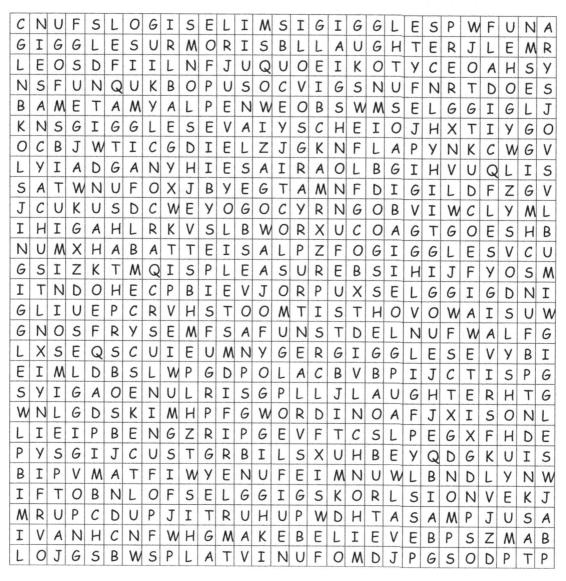

Count the number of times each word appears and write the number next to it for the answer!

SMILES _____
MAKE BELIEVE _____
GIGGLES _____
PLEASUR E _____
FUN _____
LAUGHTER _____

CIRCLE THE TWO IDENTICAL FACES!

'SOCK MONKEY' IN ANY LANGUAGE SPELLS FUN!

Draw a line to match each word to its language.

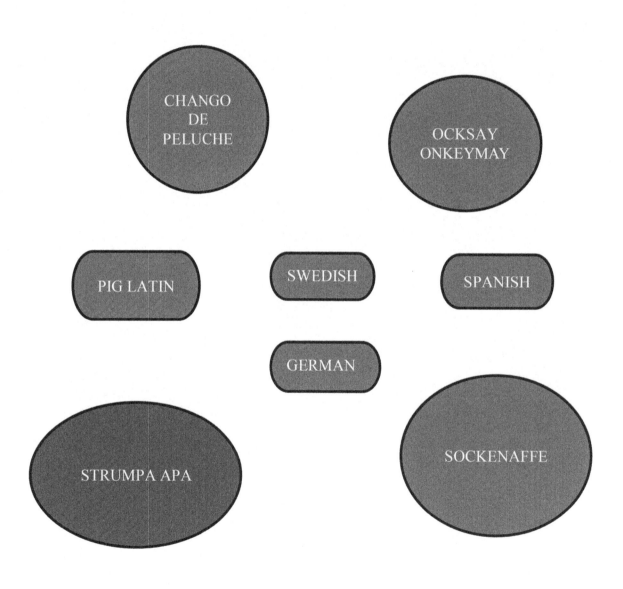

COLOR ERIC AND HANNA!

Eric & Hanna are two super-sized sock monkeys resident at the Stockholm Inn in Rockford, IL. They were created by the Sock Monkey Lady and dressed in colorful Swedish folk costumes--created sock monkey style--in honor of John Nelson who was a Swedish immigrant.

DRAW SOCKEY

USE THE GRID AS A GUIDE
AND DRAW SOCKEY'S IMAGE IN THE BOX BELOW:

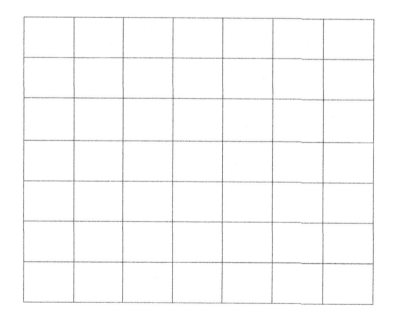

FINISH DRAWING
SOCKELLA

Sockella is missing her eyes, eyelashes, and nose! Add those attributes and any others. Sock monkey facial attributes can also include freckles, eye-brows, smile lines--even a wart if witch-like features are desired.

PLAYGROUND FUN

WHEN SOCKEY WOKE _____ ON SATURDAY, THE _____ WAS SHINING. HE SCAMPERED OUT OF HIS WARM _____ SO HE COULD BE AT THE PLAYGROUND BY_____. HE ATE A BUNCH OF _____ FOR NOURISHMENT AND_____ALL THE WAY TO THE PARK.

SOCKEY _____THE PLAYGROUND. WHEN HE FIRST GOT THERE HE CLIMBED THE TALLEST _____ WITH GLEE AND SLID DOWN A LONG CURVY_____ ON HIS RED-BUM. THEN HE RAN OVER TO THE _____ AND SWUNG VERY HIGH, HIS TAIL_____ AND UNCURLING AS HIS GANGLY LEGS PUMPED BACK AND FORTH. WHEN HE WAS DANGLING UPSIDE DOWN FROM THE TOP RUNG OF THE MONKEY BARS, HE SAW HIS_____, SOCKELLA. THEY TEETERED ON THE_____AND BOUNCED UNTIL THEIR SEAMS BEGAN TO POP. THEY PLAYED FOLLOW THE LEADER, SOCKELLA LEADING FIRST. WHEN IT WAS SOCKEY'S TURN, THEY DASHED TO THE_____AND HE AND SOCKELLA CLIMBED TO THE TOP OF THE TOWER WHERE THEY PEEKED FROM A_____AND IMAGINED DEFENDING THEIR MAGICAL KINGDOM FROM A_____THAT BREATHED_____.

WITH THEIR CHEEKS AGLOW AND SMILES_____, SOCKEY AND SOCKELLA WERE JOINED BY OTHER_____. THEY ALL HAD SOCKTASTIC FUN PLAYING _____AND KICK THE_____. SOCKEY DIDN'T WANT THIS DAY TO EVER_____, BUT_____FLEW BY AND SOCKEY FINALLY HAD TO GO_____. SOCKELLA SAID SHE WOULD_____AWAY WITHOUT HIM AND HE SAID HE WOULD MISS HER, TOO. THEY BOTH PROMISED TO MEET AT THE_____TOMORROW AND MADE A PACT TO BE FOREVER_____MATES.

PLAYGROUND KEY

1	2	3
4	5	6
7	8	9
10	11	12
13	14	15
16	17	18
19	20	21
22	23	24
25	26	27

COLOR SOCKEY'S PLAYSCAPE

COLOR SOCKEY HAVING FUN!

SYMBOLS & SOCKS

Nelson Knitting Company was located across from the Illinois Central Railroad. For many years hobos would come to their door and would be given a fresh pair of socks. Hobos would often write symbols on places such as sidewalks, buildings, and fences as a means of communicating information to other hobos about areas they were entering.

Place the number on the line in each square that tells the meaning of the symbol. Try your own hand at drawing the symbol for 'free socks' in honor of this secret language and the Red-Heel Sock Monkey Tradition.

1 - A KIND OLD LADY LIVES HERE
2 - GOOD PLACE TO CATCH A TRAIN
3 - GOOD PLACE TO HANG OUT
4 - FRESH WATER AND SAFE CAMPSITE
5 - DRAW YOUR OWN 'FREE SOCKS' SYMBOL

6 - CAMP HERE
7 - WARNING: BARKING DOG
8 - THIS IS NOT A SAFE PLACE
9 - IF YOU ARE SICK, THEY WILL
    CARE FOR YOU HERE

HELP SOCKEY'S FRIENDS FIND THEIR WAY TO THE TILT-A-WHIRL

TRACE A PATH
TO HELP SOCKEY'S PAL
FIND HIS SNACK

MAZE

KEYBOARD FUN!

Take monkeying around to another level.
Express your imagination with
keyboard art and create a sock monkey pal!
Then double-dare and key a magical playscape!

THE END

BRAINY ANSWERS

TRUE OR FALSE

1 - True
2 - True

SOCK MONKEY PARTS

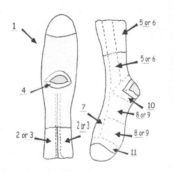

DOT TO DOT

MULTIPLE CHOICE

1-B	8-D
2-C	9-B
3-B	10-B
4-C	11-E
5-C	12-F
6-B	13-C
7-C	14-C

RIDDLE FUN!

1-Monkey
2-Retailer
3-Ape-ron

the MONKEY BUZZ!

```
B S O C K M O N K E Y S   N       T H
I G           E L B A G G U H     R   H O       Y
G G                         Y         E A D     Y       S
R O C K F O R D I L L I N O I S     A D       N       O
O I                     D A S           Y C   S T U     C
S N N I S E I D D U B N D       U       R O   U F F     K
N E S C           K N         E           O   F         P
A S N O T T U B   Y E I   U   R               E D       E
G T U N I R       S L I N           M P       S         N
I N   U I R     M I R A     M   M S           L         D
N A E   H       O     F A   O     M S   B     I         O
A N C H A T     D O   L H   S S   S E   D R O C   I     U
H E T H L   S I   R     E   S I   S E   D R     T       S
E S I I M E   E       L P E S B   I   R     O   L E     E
T H A E L   Y     A       Y I O       N   E L V L E     L
I       I M     A   G N       R C   A   N   T A S R     B
M       E A         N     O K     V S     O C F O S     A
E       T S       O             K   N T   O F C F O     E
  E         O S E D A M O N A H A H   A     B T   H   C L
S   O L B O R N I N T H E U S A A F   S     Y   O H G   V
  Y N A P M O C G N I T T I N K N O S L E N
```

FIND EIGHT FUN THINGS TO DO AT A PLAYGROUND

		C	R	A	W	L	J
		L			S		U
S	L	I	D	E	P		M
W		M			I		P
I		B	O	U	N	C	E
N							
G	H	A	N	G			

RAISE THE MONKEY BAR

SOCKPENDOUS
SOCKTASTIC
SOCKSILLYUMPTUOUS
SOCKITIZE
SOCKULENT
SOCKSATIONAL

PLAYSCAPES OFTEN INCLUDE GREEN SPACES

BASEBALL
TAG
SACK RACES
SOCCER
TOUCH FOOTBALL
BADMINTON
VOLLEYBALL
BLINDMAN'S BLUFF
CARTWHEELS
HIDE AND SEEK

FIND THE DIFFERENCES

MONKEY SHINES!

FUN 19
GIGGLES 16
SMILES 4
LAUGHTER 3
MAKE BELIEVE 2
PLEASURE 1

'SOCK MONKEY' IN ANY LANGUAGE SPELLS FUN!

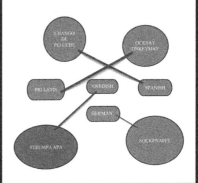

CIRCLE IDENTICAL FACES

DRAW SOCKEY

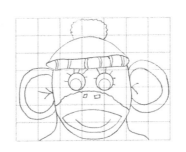

PLAYGROUND FUN

15, 10, 20, 7, 18, 24

26, 19, 27, 21, 22, 23, 2, 25, 17, 13, 14

4, 5, 11, 9, 6, 12, 8, 1, 16, 3

SYMBOLS & SOCKS

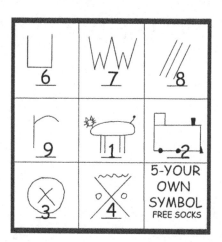

TILT-A-WHIRL MAZE

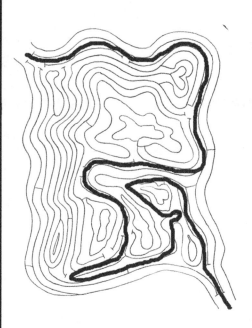

SNACK MAZE

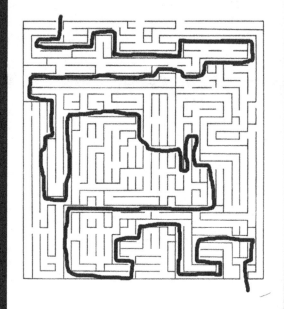

Other Books by Dee Lindner
Also Available:

Monkey Love
Friends Knock Your Socks Off
Sew Cute and Collectible Sock Monkeys
Sock Monkeys: Coloring Book
Sock Monkeys: Summer Fun Coloring Book
Sock Monkeys: America's Love Story
Sock Monkeys: Thready Wisdom
Sock Monkeys and You: On Your *Sockpendous* Day
Sock Monkeys and You: On Your *Socksational* Day
Starring Sock Monkeys: Sing & Smile
Sock Monkeys, Sock Monkeys, Sock Monkeys, Activity Book

&

Going, Going, Gone! Co-written as A. N. Charles—
An auction series cozy mystery with a sock monkey moment!

SockMonkeyLady.Com   NickVerriet.Com

Made in the USA
Monee, IL
26 December 2022

23402312R00031